Introduction

Parents and educators know too well how difficult it is to introduce children to the life of Jesus. Our adult words and preoccupations can be either too complex or too simplistic. We might embellish the story to astound the reader and perhaps miss the mystery of Jesus' character. Or we limit ourselves to a dry but factual account and perhaps hide the essence of his life.

This book has been created by parents with the help of a scripture scholar, a teacher, several catechists and Napoli, the artist. Their purpose is to help parents and children discover Jesus alive today.

A Child's Life of Jesus is a picture book. Children like pictures and know how to read them, often better than adults. A pose, a gesture, or a symbol reveals the depth of a personality to them better than words. They go beyond the image and we must allow them the joy of this personal discovery.

Sometimes they also like to see through their parents' eyes. That's why Napoli chose Bethlehem, Nazareth, Jerusalem and the countryside of Galilee and Samaria for inspiration; that's why his scenes are more suggestive and symbolic than descriptive. Sometimes they are even a bit difficult in order to convey more than an anecdote.

A Child's Life of Jesus is taken from the gospel. The imporant ideas are offered in simple wording without sacrificing their richness. Children appreciate and remember simple sentences; they like to repeat them or have them repeated by their friends. As such it becomes a form of meditation.

But the book does not contain the whole gospel, only some of the major events of the life of Jesus. Children become lost in too much detail. They comprehend more through their own inner stories than through the accumulation of details weighing down their memories. So each page gives the essential element of an event in Jesus' life and the wording which conveys its meaning.

Page by page children will find revealed the person of Jesus and the work of his salvation, his goal of love and his presence today.

The Editors

Here is the land of Jesus. Explanations for a more thorough understanding and use of the book are found on pages 38 and 39.

It's Christmas! The day Jesus was born

Joseph and Mary are traveling
  to Bethlehem.
They find no room to stay in that night
so they take shelter in a stable.

The moment of birth has come.

Mary brings her baby, Jesus,
  into the world.
She wraps him in loose cloth
and uses a manger
full of straw as a bed.

Glory to God, peace and joy on earth for all people.

Jesus in Nazareth

Now
Mary and Joseph are at home
in a town called Nazareth
in Galilee.

This is the town where Jesus grows up.

Joyfully
his parents watch as he grows
to become a man.

He works
like all the people of his village.

God sends his son

On the banks of the River Jordan
a man named John the Baptist
waits for the savior.

He teaches about the savior saying:
    Someone will come
    who is more important than I am.

And one day, Jesus arrives from Nazareth.
John points to him and says:
    God told me,
    This is Jesus, my beloved son.
    And I say to you,
    Go and follow him.

Jesus calls his friends

Jesus is on the shore of Lake Galilee.
He sees two brothers, Simon and Andrew.
They are fishermen.
And they are throwing their nets
   into the water.

Jesus says to them,
"Come, follow me."
They leave their nets
and follow him right away.

A little further
Jesus calls James and John
and asks them to follow him.
Jesus calls even more men,
twelve of them altogether.
These are the apostles
who will follow Jesus everywhere
and live with him.

Jesus welcomes everyone

Often in the evening
when the sun sets
the people living in the town
crowd around the door of the house
where Jesus is staying.

Jesus tells the good news to all.
"God wants us to be happy with him."
They bring him the sick
and Jesus cures them.

Jesus loves children

Mothers want to show
their children to Jesus.
But people try to keep the little children away.
Then Jesus becomes angry and says,
"Let the children come to me."
He takes them on his knees
and kisses them.

The words of Jesus

Many people love to listen to Jesus.
One day he climbs to the top
of a hill with them.
Then he tells them:

Blessed are the poor,
Blessed are the gentle;
God loves them.

Blessed
are those who hunger for fairness;
they will find it.

Blessed
are those who forgive;
they shall be forgiven.

Blessed
are those who work for peace;
they are the children of God.

Jesus in the country

Jesus walks a lot
with his friends.
They walk from village to village
where people wait to hear him.

When he passes through the countryside
he admires the flowers in the fields,
the birds in the sky,
the flocks on the hills.

Jesus invited to Lazarus' home

Jesus often comes to the house
of his friend Lazarus
in the town of Bethany.
He eats with him
and with his sisters, Martha and Mary.
He is always happy
to spend a while
in the homes of those who invite him.

Many express faith in Jesus

One day,
men bring a sick person
who cannot walk
to Jesus.

Jesus sees their faith;
he says to the paralyzed man,
"Any evil you have done,
I forgive you."
Some murmur,
"He has no right to say that.
Only God can forgive sins."

Jesus understands what they are thinking.
He says to them,
    You will see
    God has given me the power
    to heal and to forgive.
Then he turns to the sick man and says,
"Rise up and return home."
Right away the man gets up and walks.
All are amazed.
They have never seen anything like it.
They sing the glory of God.

A Roman soldier
comes looking for Jesus
and says to him,
"Sir, my servant is sick."

Jesus answers,
"I will go heal him."

The soldier replies:
    I am not good enough for you
    to come to my home.
    Speak only a word
    and my servant will be healed.

Jesus admires this stranger's faith.
He says to those around him:
    I have never seen
    such strong faith among you.
    I assure you,
    in all the world's countries
    many will believe in me.

Then he says to the soldier:
    Go. What you believe has happened.
    Your servant is healed.

Jesus prays

Often
Jesus goes to a place to be alone
to pray to God his father.

Sometimes
he spends the whole night
praying.

Jesus teaches us to pray

One day while Jesus prays,
his friends approach him
and say,
"Teach us to pray."

Jesus answers them,
    When you pray, say:

Our Father
who are in heaven,
blessed is your name,
your kingdom come,
your will be done
on earth as in heaven...

The Reign of God

One day Jesus says
to the many people who are listening to him:

How can you understand the reign of God
and how can I explain it to you?
The Reign of God
is like a tiny seed;
a farmer plants it
in the garden.
The seed grows
into a tree
where the birds of the sky
sit on its branches.

The Reign of God
means living all together with God.

20

God loves everyone

To help understand
how much God loves us
Jesus tells this story:

> The person who watches the lambs
> only to earn money
> is not a true shepherd.

When that person sees a wolf
coming to kill the lambs,
he runs away and leaves
the lambs alone.

The good shepherd
doesn't abandon his lambs.
I am like the good shepherd;
I give my life for you all.

Jesus says something very important

One evening while Jesus is speaking with his friends,
he tells them something very important:

Love one another
as I love you.
All people will know that you are my friends
if you love one another.

Jesus feeds a large crowd

Many people are with Jesus this day.
Evening comes and they have had
    nothing to eat.
Jesus says to his friends:
    I feel bad
    for all these people.
    What are they going to eat?

A young boy has five loaves of bread
    and two fish.
He brings them to Jesus.
Jesus has them distributed
    among all the people.

Something extraordinary happens.
There are more than 5000 people there,
and all eat as much as they want.

I am the bread of life

The following day Jesus leaves.
The people look for him
and when they find him,
Jesus says to them:
        You are looking for me
        because yesterday I fed you well.
        I have another kind of bread for you;
        it's the bread that gives life.

Then the people say to him,
"Give us that kind of bread forever."
He answers,
"I am this bread that gives life."

Many leave because
they don't understand
what Jesus means.

Some people throw stones at Jesus

When Jesus speaks
many people listen to him.
He says some things
that are hard to understand
and make some people unhappy.

They don't believe
Jesus is the son of God.
One day they throw stones at him.
But Jesus escapes.

Peter understands who Jesus really is

Jesus says to his friends:
    Many people don't know who I am.
    But you, do you know me well?

Peter answers without hesitating:
    You are the Christ,
    the son of the living God.

Jesus says to him:
    You are blessed, Peter.
    God has taught you who I am.

Jesus goes to Jerusalem

**Passover
the greatest Jewish holyday
is coming soon.**

**There are many people
on the road
going to Jerusalem
for the holyday.
Jesus knows he has enemies
in that city.
But he decides to go there anyway.**

The feast of Passover

When Jesus gets close to Jerusalem,
those who have come there for Passover
spread their coats on the road
to make a carpet for him.

They also cut large branches
from the palm trees

and lay them on the road
in front of him.

In their joy everyone cries out,
"Praise God; blessed is the one
    who's coming."

Jesus shares bread and wine

On the first evening of Passover
while eating with his friends
Jesus takes bread,
thanks God, and shares the bread.
He gives a piece to each person
    and says,
"Take; this is my body given for you."

Then he takes wine,
thanks God,
and gives it to his friends
    and says,
"This is my blood given for all."

He then tells them
to do this in his memory.

Jesus is arrested

At night after the meal
Jesus goes up on a hill
among some olive trees.
He prays to God his father.
But his apostles fall asleep.

He feels alone, forgotten.
Soldiers come and arrest him.
His enemies judge him.
He is condemned to death.

Jesus gives his life

Jesus dies on the cross.
He gives his life
for all people.
Father, I put my life
in your hands.

But do not look for Jesus among the dead.
Jesus is alive forever. Alleluia!

On the shore of the lake

Peter, John and their companions
have fished all night.
They haven't caught anything.
As they return in the morning
they hear someone shout
from the bank,

Have you caught any fish?
Throw the net to your right
and you will find some.

Then John says to Peter,
"It's the Lord Jesus."
And Peter joyfully jumps into the water
to go meet Jesus as quickly as possible.
When all have returned to the bank,
they see a fire of coals.
On top of it are fish and bread.
And Jesus says to them,
"Come, eat."

Pentecost

On the day we call Pentecost
Peter and those whom Jesus had chosen
receive God's Spirit.
And the Spirit of God gives them
great strength and joy.
Then Peter announces the great news
to everyone:
    Jesus is alive;
    he is truly the Son of God.

Jesus is with us

Since that day
Jesus' friends go out into the whole world
and tell all people:

God loves us.
Jesus is alive.
He is with us every day.

To better understand and use this book

The Land of Jesus

The country in which Jesus lived is called Palestine. It is next to the Mediterranean Sea. It is not very big—smaller than the state of Vermont. You can drive across it in a few hours. The River Jordan runs through Palestine, which is divided into three provinces: Galilee in the north, Samaria in the middle, and Judea in the south. Palestine's a hot country where the sun shines a lot. It almost never rains, so water is rare and precious. But sometimes storms make the wind blow very hard. The ground is dry and covered with pebbles. However, one can find a few trees—such as olive, fig and sycamore.

The Time of Jesus

In Jesus' time the inhabitants of this country were *farmers* who grew barley, wheat, and grapes; *fishermen* who fished Palestine's lakes; and *shepherds*, whose sheep roamed the hillsides.

The houses were quite small and stood very close to one another. They did not have roofs like today's homes, but had terraces where people sat in the evenings taking advantage of the cool night air. Men and women dressed in long wrap-around clothes. They walked everywhere, but sometimes traveled on a donkey, for in those days there were no trains, cars, or even bicycles.

The people liked to talk a lot among themselves and tell stories. They had no books, newspapers, radio or television. Jesus told many stories like the one about the shepherd; we call these parables.

The People of Jesus

Jesus was one of an ancient people called the Jews. They were the only people on earth who, for many years, understood that God is one, faithful, just, and all powerful. It was among these people that God chose to have his son born. For many years, through their joy and suffering, God prepared the Jews to welcome Jesus. The entire Jewish people were expecting someone without knowing precisely who it would be. When Jesus was born, another people, the Romans, ruled Palestine, and the Jews were very unhappy. But they hoped that God would help them and that they would be able to conquer their enemies. They believed that a Savior, promised to them long ago, would deliver them from the Romans.

Jesus was the promised Savior, the son of God. Not everyone understood this, for Jesus did not come to lead his people to victory over the Romans, but to tell all people of all times that God loved them.

Jewish Customs

Passover: For the Jews this was the greatest and oldest holyday. On this day every family ate the same meal: roast lamb and unleavened bread. The three-day holyday reminded them that God liberated them and led them out of Egypt where they were slaves.

Pentecost: This was also a Jewish holyday which celebrated harvesting the wheat. It was a time to thank God for all he had given his people.

The Cross: When the Romans condemned a Jew to die, they nailed the person on two pieces of crossed wood. Many people, like Jesus, suffered terribly dying this way.

Jesus' Friends: Jesus asked twelve of his friends to leave their families and jobs in order to live with him and follow him everywhere.

Lazarus: He was a friend of Jesus who wasn't always with him. He lived in the town of Bethany with his sisters Martha and Mary.

The Characters:

Mary: This is Jesus' mother.

Joseph: This is Mary's husband. He was a carpenter. When Jesus was little, Joseph took care of him the way all fathers do.

John the Baptist: He lived alone in a deserted place in Palestine where the River Jordan flows into the Dead Sea. Like the rest of his people, John the Baptist was waiting for the Savior. He was a holy man who spoke well about God and many people came to see him.

The Roman Soldier: In Jesus' time, Roman soldiers occupied Palestine. The Jews thought of them as foreign pagans and wouldn't enter their homes. That's why the Roman soldier, whose servant was sick, didn't dare ask Jesus to come to his home.

The Places:

Bethlehem: This was the little village in Judea where Jesus was born. Joseph and Mary (who was expecting her baby) travelled a long way from Nazareth to Bethlehem. They were obeying an order of the Roman emperor.

Nazareth: This was the little town in Galilee where Jesus grew up. Galilee was the prettiest region in Palestine. Things were greener there because of its many flowers and trees. Jesus liked it a lot. Almost all his friends came from Galilee. It is where he spoke and travelled most. After leaving his parents he lived in Capernaum on the shore of Lake Galilee.

Jerusalem: This was the biggest city in Palestine. It was built in Judea on top of a hill. There the Jews built the Temple where they worshipped God. Like all his people Jesus often went to Jerusalem, and that is where he died.

Lake Galilee: The Jordan River runs through it. In this lake there are a great number of fish which the fishermen catch with nets from their boats.

Bethany: This is the little village near Jerusalem where Jesus' friends, Lazarus and his sisters Martha and Mary, lived. Jesus often visited them in their home.

This book was produced by Danielle Monneron working with the editors of Pomme d'Api: Yves and Marie-Josèphe Beccaria, Jean-Claude Cardon, Anne-Marie de Besombes, Jeanne-Marie Faure, Jacqueline Quéniart; and with the cooperation of René Berthier, Joseph Dheilly, Pierre Dufourcq, Charles Ehlinger, Jean-Claude Eslin, Christiane Gaud, Hervé Stéphan, Bernard Violle.

Table of contents

Nihil Obstat: M. Tolu, pss

Imprimatur: Most Reverend M. Berrar
               Bishop of Paris

A Child's Life of Jesus was originally published as *La Vie de Jesus*. © copyright 1971, Pomme d'Api. Editions du Centurion, Paris, France.

© 1990 by Ave Maria Press, Notre Dame, IN 46556

International Standard Book Number: 0-87793-415-0

Library of Congress Catalog Card Number: 89-81355

Printed and bound in the United States of America.